SIR THOMAS WYATT Poems

Sir Thomas Wyatt was born in K[...]
John's College, Cambridge. He se[...]
in Europe but was imprisoned and almost executed for his close
relationship with Anne Boleyn. On his release, Wyatt became
Sheriff of Kent and later Ambassador to Spain, and died 1542
from a fever caught on a diplomatic mission.

Alice Oswald lives in Devon and is married with three children.
Dart, her second volume, won the T. S. Eliot Prize in 2002. Her
third collection, *Woods etc*, won the Geoffrey Faber Memorial
Prize 2006.

SIR THOMAS WYATT

Poems selected by ALICE OSWALD

faber and faber

First published in 2008
by Faber and Faber Limited
3 Queen Square London WC1N 3AU

Photoset by RefineCatch Ltd, Bungay, Suffolk
Printed in England by CPI Bookmarque, Croydon

A CIP record for this book
is available from the British Library

ISBN 978–0–571–23229–1

10 9 8 7 6 5 4 3 2 1

Contents

FROM THE BLAGE MS

Introduction

Born at Allington Castle in Kent in 1503. Presented at Henry VIII's Court age thirteen. Married Elizabeth Brooke in 1520 and had two children by her but subsequently divorced. Travelled to French Court in 1526, with Sir Thomas Cheyney, then to Italy in 1527. In 1535 he was knighted; in 1536 he was arrested, and witnessed executions of Anne Boleyn and several friends. Began a relationship with Elizabeth Darrell in 1537 and was sent the same year to negotiate with Emperor Charles V in Spain. 1539: recalled to England. 1540: arrested and then pardoned. 1542: died en route to Falmouth to meet Spanish envoy.

We think of Wyatt as a love poet, but it might be more helpful to think of him as a fear poet – a poet of disquiet. Wyatt the love poet was not so very different from his contemporaries: Blage, Bryan, Boleyn, Knyvet, Surrey. They were all acquaintances, all members of Henry VIII's court. Their poems, read mainly by each other, spoke a kind of courtly love-patter, a language of postures and polite images taken straight from Chaucer:

> At moost mischief
> I suffre grief
> for of relief
> syns I have none
> my lute and I
> continuelly
> shall us apply
> to sigh and moan . . .

Listening to the gloomy strumming of that kind of poem, you might well decide not to read any further.

But Wyatt the fear poet is different. His clearest expression comes in the poem given here on page 69:

> Stond who so list upon the slipper toppe

of courtes estates, and lett me heare rejoyce;
and use me quyet without lett or stoppe,
unknowen in courte, that hath such brackish joyes.
In hidden place, so lett my dayes forthe passe,
that when my years be done, withouten noyse,
I may dye aged after the common trace.
For him death greep'the right hard by the croppe
that is moche knowen of other, and of himself alas,
doth dye unknowen, dazed with dredful face.

This poem, written two years before Wyatt's death, is his help-
less escape-wish, in which, after a lifetime of service to the king,
he asks to give up, to hide, to become: 'unknown in court, that
hath such brackish joys . . .' In 1540, when he wrote it, his patron
Thomas Cromwell had recently been executed and Wyatt himself was being accused of treason. The real issue was his relationship with Elizabeth Darrell, who was a Catholic and maid
of honour to Katharine of Aragon. Wyatt was pardoned, but
one of the conditions of his release was that he leave his mistress and return to his estranged wife.

In the aftershock of these events, Wyatt was at home at
Allington – frightened, heart-broken, forced to make terms
with a wife who'd betrayed him fifteen years before. If you lean
right into the darkness of the poem, there's something hap-
pening around the word 'brackish' in line 4 – an unusual
adjective for joy, but full of meaning to anyone who knows the
murky look of tidal water. In fact the River Medway runs
alongside Wyatt's garden and is tidal as far as Maidstone. In an
earlier poem, Wyatt had written: 'Oft ye rivers, to hear my
woeful sound, have stopped your course . . .' I imagine he was
often to be found two hundred yards from his front door,
focussing his depression on the slack, sick look of highwater as
it turns.

'Stond who so list . . .' is a translated poem, made of conventional material. But once you've seen this snapshot of its
author, you can begin to feel the pressure that makes its lan-

guage work. The original poem, by Seneca, was a light, four-beat lyric, an excerpt from his play *Thyestes*. As with most choral lyric, it kept itself rooted in generalities:

> illi mors gravis incubat
> qui notus nimis omnibus
> ignotus moritur sibi . . .

In Wyatt's poem, the truism of those three lines became a terrifying replay of Cromwell's execution. Wyatt had already witnessed the executions of several of his friends and he could never shake the experience from his mind. A contemporary, visiting him in Spain shortly before this poem was written, said of him: 'Mr. Wyatt . . . doth often call to his remembrance his emprisonment in the Tower, which seemeth so to stick in his stomacke that he cannot forget it . . .' It's worth noticing that the final close-up image of the victim – 'dazed with dredful face' – is Wyatt's invention, with no counterpart in Seneca.

I once read that poem onto a tape recorder. When I played it back, I was shocked to hear not my own voice but a man's voice – a very tired, grief-stricken man, speaking as if under a great weight of earth and care. That voice (the sound of a breaking tape recorder) is now so stuck in my head, I've come to accept it as the right one for Wyatt. At any rate, it has alerted me to his lonely strangeness, where someone else might make more of his conformities.

Most of Wyatt's poetry is wired up to this anguish. His sonnets in particular can be construed as collisions between a love poem and a fear poem, and to read them well you need to read them in both registers. You need to read them light and courtly and tired and grief-stricken.

Wyatt turned to sonnet form when it became dangerous to express his love openly. In his early twenties he had fallen in love with Anne Boleyn. A story is told about him playing boules with the king. There was a disputed throw. Henry VIII held out his hand with Anne's ring on it and said, 'Wyatt, I tell thee it is mine'; to which Wyatt replied, 'And if it may like your majesty to give me leave to measure it, I hope it will be mine.' Whereupon he measured the throw with the lace and jewels he had from Anne Boleyn. But he knew when he was beaten. A few years later he was on his way to Italy to discuss Henry VIII's divorce, leaving his rival free to marry Anne.

It was in the context of that humiliating and complicated embassy that Wyatt came across Petrarch's poems. His translations, which became the first sonnets written in English, are fraught readings of Petrarch, full of the difficulty of his own position:

> And graven with diamonds, in letters plain
> There is written her fair neck round about:
> '*Noli me tangere* for Caesar's I am,
> and wild for to hold though I seem tame.'

Wyatt used Petrarch as an instrument of self-expression, the way a man might use a flute. He chose sonnets that were relevant to his own experience and then re-ordered and personalised them. In the poem above (see pages xxiii and 6), he refers obliquely to the incident at boules. But he has discoloured all Petrarch's imagery: the deer is no longer white, the antlers no longer gold, the green grass not even mentioned. He has emphatically altered the sequence of ideas and left out Petrarch's reference to the sun and the time of day, so that the action of the poem is driven inward, into the poet's mind. Where Petrarch wrote an allegory, Wyatt writes a metaphor. His translated sonnets all follow this pattern. They bring the original inside, into the distorted topography of the heart. They give more to the ear than to the eye.

Petrarch wrote in lines of eleven syllables. He deliberately gave a rough edge to his metre, in reaction against the refinements of Dante and Calvacanti. Something of this roughness comes out in Wyatt, who, like Petrarch, used a varying arrangment of long and short syllables within a ten- or eleven-syllable line.

A Wyatt sonnet is therefore a completely different thing from a Surrey/Sidney/Spenser/Shakespeare sonnet. Those writers all used iambic pentameter, whose regular repetitions of soft and strong stresses gives the line a sliding, narcotic quality, which is why it became known as 'flowing' or 'riding' verse. Wyatt used 'riding' verse in his psalms and satires and in most of his epigrams. But the dissonant, disrupted tone of his sonnets is closer in spirit to the 'stopping' verse of old English poetry, whose pattern depends on the use of the caesura in the middle of each line.

During Wyatt's lifetime and right up to the end of the sixteenth century, English poetry was in the process of fixing the rules for the riding line. It's unfortunate that when Wyatt's poetry was first published in 1557, in *Tottel's Miscellany* (fifteen years after Wyatt's death), those rules had become so fashionable that Tottel, or his editor Nicholas Grimald, altered the manuscripts to fit them.

'Then revenge you: and the next way is this,' wrote Wyatt, which Tottel changed to 'Revenge you then, the readiest way is this'. Wyatt's line contains an articulate pause at the colon. Tottel's line merely hesitates, but the expectation of the next iamb is so strong that the reader is driven forward over the comma. 'I served thee not to be forsaken', says Wyatt, catching his breath between 'thee' and 'not'. Tottel, absolutely unbreathlessly, says 'I served thee not that I should be forsaken'. Wyatt: 'and the reward little trust forever'; Tottel: 'and the reward is little trust forever'; Wyatt: 'I have seen them gentill, tame and meke'; Tottel: 'once have I seen them gentle, tame and meek'; Wyatt: 'I fley above the wind yet can I not arise'; Tottel: 'I flye aloft, yet can I not arise'. In most cases Tottel is simply adding another beat, but the effect is to censor the emotion of the line.

Wyatt didn't choose to be published. He wrote poems for circulation in manuscript among friends, which meant that his texts were never tied to a final form. Any reader was free to adjust what he found. But print is a very persuasive and fixing medium. Once Tottel had produced his *Miscellany*, the poems were locked into those versions and for three hundred years no alternative was offered. Even after the original manuscripts became available, people continued to believe, like Tottel, that their sounds had been catastrophically mismanaged. One editor, Miss Foxwell, even suggested a new form of pronunciation as a way of bringing Wyatt into line with convention.

Although it's fashionable now to approve of Wyatt's metres, English literature is creased into the iambic system and it's hard to unfold it. Hayward made 'They flee from me' the opening poem of his *Penguin Book of English Verse* (1956), but by mistake printed Tottel's version. Rebholz, who edited the most recent and widely used edition of Wyatt, despite spending eleven pages justifying the metres, still blurts out suddenly, 'Wyatt's art is not always adequate to his ideal objective' (whose ideal?) and then proceeds, exactly like Tottel, to alter the texts: 'I have amended line 3 [of 'A Lady gave me a Gift . . .' etc.] because it seems likely that the first four lines should have ten syllables'.

There's plenty to be said about stressed and unstressed syllables and the stressed and unstressed writers who count them up, but the important question (for me) is whether you hear in Wyatt a hurrying, incremental kind of music or whether you hear something more to and fro and rewinding, like birdsong – in which case the poem's overall effect is mainly made of the turnings and spaces between phrases. I think these two ways of reading are radically, even metaphysically different. To read a poem in the first way, you need a certain momentum – the meaning of the text is something flowed towards and final – and you could well be justified in editing syllables to ease the process. The second way of reading is to do with the echo and opposition of real sounds within one line. It needs to proceed much more slowly, because the centre upon which the meanings converge lies outside the language, in the pauses.

That's the way I read Wyatt. Which is why I find it helpful to see his poems in the context of the 'pausing' tradition that preceeded them.

Like liturgical music, pausing verse sets up sequences of not quite matching phrases. Between each phrase there is a hinge – a twist of the head or a cough or catch in the verse through which the poet maintains his connexion with silence. Like this:

who so list to hounte   I know, where is an hynde.
but as for me   helas   I may no more
The vayne travaill hath weried me so sore.
I am of theim   that farthest cometh behinde
Yet may I   by no means   my weried mynde
drawe from the Diere   but as she fleeth afore
faynting I folowe   I leve of therefore
sithens in a nette I seke to hold the wynde
who list her hount   I put him owte of dowbte
as well, as I   may spend his time in vain
and graven with Diamondes   in letters plain
there is written   her faier neck rounde abowte:
Noli me tangere   for Cesar's I ame
and wylde for to hold   though I seme tame

Of course this way of setting it out exaggerates the poem's bro-
kenness, whereas the conventional, joined-up version that
appears later in this selection implies a more settled, smooth-
talking, even manipulative tone. Think of the different ways an
actor might say: 'there is written her fair neck round about' and
'there is written   her fair neck round about'. It's like a verse
of Emily Dickenson – it means one thing when you include the
dashes and quite another when you remove them.

It's a matter of taste. It's impossible, even on a broken tape
recorder, to summon up Wyatt's real speaking sound. On the
one hand, he was a courtier and a diplomat and needed to move
fast through every shade of falsehood. On the other hand, what
we have left of his letters and speeches suggests that honesty (or
as he often calls it: 'Trouthe') was in his very marrow: 'I have
nothing to call upon you for but honesty honesty,' he wrote to
his son, 'the honesty that is the more godly for it is so rare and
strange'. This amphibious way of being is matched by the
absolute inconsistency of the manuscripts when it comes to
punctuation. The first few poems of the Egerton (Wyatt's own
manuscript) are peppered with dots and colons and commas
and slashes, as if someone was trying to notate every throat-

clearing and hesitation in the language. Then suddenly the effort is abandoned and we're left with pages of no punctuation, as if all the words were to be read in a monotone.

The question of Wyatt's voice and, in particular, the question of how to calibrate his pauses affect our sense of Wyatt as a character in his poems' drama. When the pause is overridden, the poet more or less controls his medium. When the pause is marked, then something other than language, something unsayable, is given space. The best Wyatt poems are complex treaties with the pause. Sometimes the line opens up and lets it through, sometimes the line closes over; but always there is this pressure, this possibility of interruption, this unstable rhythm of quiet and disquiet that constitutes the poem's action.

And disquiet, the impossibility, for a man of Wyatt's status, of finding any kind of quiet, is what he always comes back to. In his early twenties he had published a translation of Plutarch's *Quyete of Mynde*. In his late thirties he was still writing on the same theme:

'The piller pearisht is whearto I lent
the strongest staye of myne unquyet mynde . . .'

'. . . ere that I in this find peace or quietness . . .'

'Stond whoso list upon the slipper toppe
of courtes estates, and lett me heare rejoyce;
and use me quyet without lett or stoppe . . .'

It's ironic that Tottel took the 'let' and 'stop' out of Wyatt's verse, as if trying to solve metrically the conflict upon which every word is founded.

POSTSRCIPT
Wyatt died very suddenly on his way to Falmouth in 1542. He rode too fast, caught a chill and died at a friend's house in Dorset. Strangely, for a man of his status, he was buried not in his own grave, but in his host's family tomb. His mistress,

Elizabeth Darrell, whom he'd been forced to leave two years before, was living in Exeter, and I can't help wondering whether, on his way to the West Country, he decided to fake his own death to rejoin her. The beauty of that idea is that it changes the poem 'Stond who so list . . .' from a wish into a whispered decision:

> in hidden place, so lett my dayes forth passe,
> that when my yeares be done, withouten noyse,
> I maye die aged after the common trace . . .

Whether, having finally achieved some kind of 'quyet without lett or stop', Wyatt (not Tottel) then proceeded to edit his poems, it would be mad to speculate.

ALICE OSWALD

I am very grateful to: the British Library, Sir Robert Worcester, Laura Beatty, Mary Keen, Catherine Keen, James Fenton, Peter Oswald, Paul Keegan, Matthew Hollis, R. A. Rebholz, Kenneth Muir, Henry Woudhuysen and Charles Boyle.

Note on the Text

Wyatt's poems appear in a number of manuscripts. The Egerton, Wyatt's own, opens this selection; followed by the Blage, which belonged to Wyatt's friend George Blage and was not discovered until the 1960s. The Devonshire manuscript contains several poems unrecorded elsewhere as well as earlier versions of poems in the Egerton. Wyatt's poems also appear in the Arundel and Tottel manuscripts and in minor manuscripts and they come in that order in this selection.

The text of the poems is taken from the Penguin edition, edited by Rebholz (with minor amendments). Rebholz's modernised spelling and punctuation have the advantage of making the language accessible to a modern audience, but the disadvantage of allowing the poems to be skim-read, fast and prosily. To emphasise the point that the energy of a Wyatt poem is stored in the spaces not the materials of the language, this selection opens with five poems as Wyatt would have written them – in old spelling and without punctuation. My own feeling is that Wyatt in modernised spelling sounds like an outdated, reedy-voiced old man, but in his own spelling he is revolutionary and alive. Those first poems, and the prose excerpt from Wyatt's defence to the judges, give the tuning note for all the rest.

Excerpt from Wyatt's 1541 defence to the judges

Come on, now, my Lord of London, what is my abominable and vicious living? Do ye know it, or have ye heard it? I grant I do not profess chastity; but yet I use not abominations. If ye know it, tell it here, with whom and when. If ye heard it, who is your author? Have ye seen me have any harlot in my house whilst ye were in my company? Did you ever see woman so much as dine, or sup, at my table? None, but for your pleasure, the woman that was in the galley; which I assure you may well be seen; for, before you came, neither she nor any other came above the mast. But because the gentlemen took pleasure to see you entertain her, therefore they made her dine and sup with you; and they liked well your looks, your carving to Madonna, your drinking to her, and your playing under the table. Ask Mason, ask Blage – Bowes is dead – ask Wolf, that was my steward; they can tell how the gentlemen marked it, and talked of it. It was a play to them, the keeping of your bottles, that no man might drink of but yourself; and 'that the little fat priest were a jolly morsel for the Signora'. This was their talk; it is not my devise: ask other, whether I do lie.

Behold love thy power how she despiseth
My great payne how little she regardeth
The holy oth wherof she taketh no cure
Broken she hath and yet she bideth sure
Right at her ease and little she dreadeth
Wepened thou art and she vnarmed sitteth
To the disdaynfull her liff she ledeth
To me spitefull withoute cause or mesure
    Behold love

I ame in hold if pitie the meveth
Goo bend thy bowe that stony hertes breketh
And with some stroke revenge the displeasure
Of thee and him that sorrowe doeth endure
And as his lorde thee lowly entreath
    Behold love

What vaileth trouth or by it to take payne
To stryve by stedfastnes for to attayne
To be iuste and true and fle from dowblenes
Sythens all alike where rueleth craftines
Rewarded is boeth fals and plain
Sonest he spedeth that moost can fain
True meaning hert is had in disdain
Against deceipte and dowblenes
   What vaileth trouth

Decyved is he by crafty trayn
That meaneth no gile and doeth remain
Within the trapp without redresse
But for to love lo suche a maisteres
Whose crueltie nothing can refrayne
   What vaileth trouth

The longe love that in my thought doeth harbar
And in myn hert doeth kepe his residence
Into my face preseth with bold pretence
And therein campeth spreding his baner
She that me lerneth to love and suffer
And will that my trust and lustes negligence
By rayned by reason shame and reverence
With his hardiness taketh displeasure
Wherewithall vnto the hertes forrest he fleith
Leving his entreprise with payne and cry
And there him hideth and not appereth
What may I do when my maister fereth
But in the felds with him to lyve and dye
For goode is the liff ending faithfully

Who so list to hounte I know where is an hynde
But as for me helas I may no more
The vayne travaille hath weried me so sore
I ame of theim that farthest cometh behinde
Yet may I by no meanes my weried mynde
Drawe from the Diere but as she fleeth afore
Faynting I folowe I leve of therefore
Sithens in a nett I seke to hold the wynde
Who list her hount I put him owte of dowbte
As well as I may spend his tyme in vain
And graven with Diamondes in letters plain
There is written her faier neck rounde abowte
Noli me tangere for Cesars I ame
And wylde for to hold though I seme tame

Helpe me to seke for I lost it there
And if that ye have founde it ye that be here
And seke to convaye it secretely
Handell it soft and trete it tenderly
Or els it will plain and then appere
But rather restore it mannerly
Syns that I do aske it thus honestly
For to lese it it sitteth me to neere
    Helpe me to seke

Alas and is there no remedy
But have I thus lost it wilfully
I wis it was a thing all to dere
To be bestowed and wist not where
It was myn hert I pray you hertely
    Helpe me to seke

SIR THOMAS WYATT

∾

Behold, Love, thy power how she despiseth,
My great pain how little she regardeth.
The holy oath whereof she taketh no cure
Broken she hath, and yet she bideth sure
Right at her ease and little she dreadeth.
Weaponed thou art and she unarmed sitteth.
To thee disdainful her life she leadeth,
To me spiteful without cause or measure.
   Behold, Love.
I am in hold. If pity thee moveth,
Go bend thy bow that stony hearts breaketh
And with some stroke revenge the displeasure
Of thee and him that sorrow doth endure
   And, as his lord, thee lowly entreateth:
     Behold, Love.

[imitated from Petrarch, *Rime* CXXI]

3

～

What vaileth truth or by it to take pain,
To strive by steadfastness for to attain
To be just and true and flee from doubleness,
Sithens all alike, where ruleth craftiness,
Rewarded is both false and plain?
Soonest he speedeth that most can feign.
True meaning heart is had in disdain.
Against deceit and doubleness
    What vaileth truth?
Deceived is he by crafty train
That meaneth no guile and doth remain
Within the trap without redress
But for to love, lo, such a mistress
Whose cruelty nothing can refrain.
    What vaileth truth?

The long love that in my thought doth harbour
And in mine heart doth keep his residence
Into my face presseth with bold pretence
And therein campeth, spreading his banner.
She that me learneth to love and suffer
And will that my trust and lust's negligence
Be reined by reason, shame, and reverence,
With his hardiness taketh displeasure.
Wherewithal unto the heart's forest he fleeth,
Leaving his enterprise with pain and cry
And there him hideth and not appeareth.
What may I do when my master feareth,
But in the field with him to live and die?
For good is the life ending faithfully.

[imitated from Petrarch, *Rime* CXL]

Whoso list to hunt, I know where is an hind,
But as for me, helas, I may no more.
The vain travail hath wearied me so sore,
I am of them that farthest cometh behind.
Yet may I by no means my wearied mind
Draw from the deer, but as she fleeth afore
Fainting I follow. I leave off therefore
Sithens in a net I seek to hold the wind.
Who list her hunt, I put him out of doubt,
As well as I may spend his time in vain.
And graven with diamonds in letters plain
There is written her fair neck round about:
Noli me tangere for Caesar's I am
And wild for to hold though I seem tame.

[imitated from Petrarch, *Rime* CXC]

Was I never yet of your love grieved
Nor never shall while that my life doth last.
But of hating myself that date is past,
And tears continual sore have me wearied.
I will not yet in my grave be buried
Nor on my tomb your name yfixed fast
As cruel cause that did the spirit soon haste
From th'unhappy bones by great sighs stirred.
Then if an heart of amorous faith and will
May content you without doing grief,
Please it you so to this to do relief.
If otherwise ye seek for to fulfil
Your disdain, ye err and shall not as ye ween,
And ye yourself the cause thereof hath been.

[imitated from Petrarch, *Rime* LXXXII]

~

Each man me telleth I change most my device,
And on my faith me think it good reason
To change purpose like after the season.
For in every case to keep still one guise
Is meet for them that would be taken wise;
And I am not of such manner condition
But treated after a diverse fashion,
And thereupon my diverseness doth rise.
But you that blame this diverseness most,
Change you no more, but still after one rate
Treat ye me well and keep ye in the same state;
And while with me doth dwell this wearied ghost,
My word nor I shall not be variable
But always one, your own both firm and stable.

If amorous faith in heart unfeigned,
A sweet languor, a great lovely desire,
If honest will kindled in gentle fire,
If long error in a blind maze chained,
If in my visage each thought depainted,
Or else in my sparkling voice lower or higher
Which now fear, now shame, woefully doth tire,
If a pale colour which love hath stained,
If to have another than myself more dear,
If wailing or sighing continually,
With sorrowful anger feeding busily,
If burning afar off and freezing near
Are cause that by love myself I destroy,
Yours is the fault and mine the great annoy.

[imitated from Petrarch, *Rime* CCXXIV]

Farewell, Love, and all thy laws forever.
Thy baited hooks shall tangle me no more.
Senec and Plato call me from thy lore
To perfect wealth my wit for to endeavour.
In blind error when I did persever,
Thy sharp repulse that pricketh ay so sore
Hath taught me to set in trifles no store
And scape forth since liberty is lever.
Therefore farewell. Go trouble younger hearts
And in me claim no more authority.
With idle youth go use thy property
And thereon spend thy many brittle darts:
For hitherto though I have lost all my time,
Me lusteth no longer rotten boughs to climb.

My heart I gave thee, not to do it pain;
But to preserve, it was to thee taken.
I served thee, not to be forsaken,
But that I should be rewarded again.
I was content thy servant to remain
But not to be paid under this fashion.
Now since in thee is none other reason,
Displease thee not if that I do refrain,
Unsatiate of my woe and thy desire,
Assured by craft to excuse thy fault.
But since it please thee to feign a default,
Farewell, I say, parting from the fire:
For he that believeth bearing in hand,
Plougheth in water and soweth in the sand.

[imitated from Serafino, *Opere* f.151]

~

For to love her for her looks lovely
My heart was set in thought right firmly,
Trusting by truth to have had redress.
But she hath made another promise
And hath given me leave full honestly.
Yet do I not rejoice it greatly
For on my faith I loved too surely.
But reason will that I do cease
   For to love her.

Since that in love the pains been deadly,
Methink it best that readily
I do return to my first address,
For at this time too great is the press
And perils appear too abundantly
   For to love her.

       [possibly imitated from Marot]

Help me to seek for I lost it there
And if that ye have found it, ye that be here,
And seek to convey it secretly,
Handle it soft and treat it tenderly
Or else it will plain and then appair.
But rather restore it mannerly
Since that I do ask it thus honestly,
For to lose it it sitteth me too near.
    Help me to seek.
Alas and is there no remedy
But have I thus lost it wilfully?
Iwis it was a thing all too dear
To be bestowed and wist not where:
It was mine heart. I pray you heartily
    Help me to seek.

[possibly imitated from Serafino]

13

∾

Go, burning sighs, unto the frozen heart.
Go break the ice which pity's painful dart
Might never pierce; and if mortal prayer
In heaven may be heard, at least I desire
That death or mercy be end of my smart.
Take with thee pain whereof I have my part
And eke the flame from which I cannot start
And leave me then in rest I you require.
   Go, burning sighs.
I must go work I see by craft and art
For truth and faith in her is laid apart.
Alas, I cannot therefore assail her
With pitiful plaint and scalding fire
That out of my breast doth strainably start.
   Go, burning sighs.

[imitated from Petrarch, *Rime* CLIII]

It may be good, like it who list.
But I do doubt. Who can me blame?
For oft assured yet have I missed
And now again I fear the same.
The windy words, the eyes' quaint game
Of sudden change maketh me aghast.
For dread to fall I stand not fast.

Alas, I tread an endless maze
That seek to accord two contraries
And hope still, and nothing haze,
Imprisoned in liberties,
As one unheard and still that cries,
Always thirsty and yet nothing I taste.
For dread to fall I stand not fast.

Assured I doubt I be not sure.
And should I trust to such surety
That oft hath put the proof in ure
And never hath found it trusty?
Nay sir in faith it were great folly.
And yet my life thus I do waste:
For dread to fall I stand not fast.

∾

Some fowls there be that have so perfect sight
Against the sun their eyes for to defend
And some because the light doth them offend
Do never 'pear but in the dark or night.
Other rejoice that see the fire bright
And ween to play in it as they do pretend
And find the contrary of it that they intend.
Alas, of that sort I may be by right,
For to withstand her look I am not able
And yet can I not hide me in no dark place,
Remembrance so followeth me of that face.
So that with teary eyen, swollen and unstable,
My destiny to behold her doth me lead,
Yet do I know I run into the gleed.

[imitated from Petrarch, *Rime* xix]

16

Because I have thee still kept fro lies and blame
And to my power always have I thee honoured,
Unkind tongue, right ill hast thou me rendered
For such desert to do me wreak and shame.
In need of succour most when that I am
To ask reward, then standest thou like one afeard,
Alway most cold; and if thou speak toward,
It is as in dream, unperfect and lame.
And ye salt tears, against my will each night
That are with me when fain I would be alone,
Then are ye gone when I should make my moan.
And you so ready sighs to make me shright,
Then are ye slack when that ye should outstart
And only my look declareth my heart.

[imitated from Petrarch, *Rime* XLIX]

∾

I find no peace and all my war is done.
I fear and hope, I burn and freeze like ice.
I fly above the wind yet can I not arise.
And naught I have and all the world I seize on.
That looseth nor locketh holdeth me in prison
And holdeth me not, yet can I scape no wise,
Nor letteth me live nor die at my device
And yet of death it giveth me occasion.
Without eyen I see and without tongue I plain.
I desire to perish and yet I ask health.
I love another and thus I hate myself.
I feed me in sorrow and laugh in all my pain.
Likewise displeaseth me both death and life
And my delight is causer of this strife.

[imitated from Petrarch, *Rime* cxxxiv]

Though I myself be bridled of my mind,
Returning me backward by force express,
If thou seek honour to keep thy promise,
Who may thee hold, my heart, but thou thyself unbind?
Sigh then no more since no way man may find
Thy virtue to let though that frowardness
Of fortune me holdeth; and yet as I may guess,
Though other be present, thou art not all behind.
Suffice it then that thou be ready there
At all hours, still under the defence
Of time, truth, and love to save thee from offence,
Crying I burn in a lovely desire
With my dear master's that may not follow,
Whereby his absence turneth him to sorrow.

[imitated from Petrarch, *Rime* xcviii]

My galley charged with forgetfulness
Thorough sharp seas in winter nights doth pass
'Tween rock and rock; and eke mine enemy, alas,
That is my lord, steereth with cruelness;
And every oar a thought in readiness
As though that death were light in such a case.
An endless wind doth tear the sail apace
Of forced sighs and trusty fearfulness.
A rain of tears, a cloud of dark disdain
Hath done the wearied cords great hindrance,
Wreathed with error and eke with ignorance.
The stars be hid that led me to this pain.
Drowned is reason that should me comfort
And I remain despairing of the port.

[imitated from Petrarch, *Rime* CLXXXIX]

~

Ever mine hap is slack and slow in coming,
Desire increasing, mine hope uncertain,
That leave it or wait it doth me like pain
And tiger-like swift it is in parting.
Alas, the snow shall be black and scalding,
The sea waterless, fish in the mountain,
The Thames shall return back into his fountain,
And where he rose the sun shall take lodging
Ere that I in this find peace or quietness
Or that Love or my lady rightwisely
Leave to conspire again me wrongfully.
And if that I have after such bitterness
Anything sweet, my mouth is out of taste,
That all my trust and travail is but waste.

[imitated from Petrarch, *Rime* LVII]

～

Love and Fortune and my mind, rememb'rer
Of that that is now with that that hath been,
Do torment me so that I very often
Envy them beyond all measure.
Love slayeth mine heart. Fortune is depriver
Of all my comfort. The foolish mind then
Burneth and plaineth as one that seldom
Liveth in rest, still in displeasure.
My pleasant days, they fleet away and pass,
But daily yet the ill doth change into the worse,
And more than the half is run of my course.
Alas, not of steel but of brickle glass
I see that from mine hand falleth my trust,
And all my thoughts are dashed into dust.

[imitated from Petrarch, *Rime* CXXIV]

How oft have I, my dear and cruel foe,
With those your eyes for to get peace and truce
Proffered you mine heart! But you do not use
Among so high things to cast your mind so low.
If any other look for it, as ye trow,
Their vain weak hope doth greatly them abuse.
And thus I disdain that that ye refuse:
It was once mine, it can no more be so.
If I then it chase, nor it in you can find
In this exile no manner of comfort,
Nor live alone, nor, where he is called, resort,
He may wander from his natural kind.
So shall it be great hurt unto us twain
And yours the loss and mine the deadly pain.

[imitated from Petrarch, *Rime* xxi]

23

~

Madam, withouten many words
Once I am sure ye will or no
And if ye will then leave your bourds
And use your wit and shew it so

And with a beck ye shall me call.
And if of one that burneth alway
Ye have any pity at all
Answer him fair with yea or nay.

If it be yea I shall be fain.
If it be nay friends as before.
Ye shall another man obtain
And I mine own and yours no more.

[imitated from a madrigal by Bonifacio]

bourds – games, jesting

They flee from me that sometime did me seek
With naked foot stalking in my chamber.
I have seen them gentle, tame and meek
That now are wild and do not remember
That sometime they put themself in danger
To take bread at my hand; and now they range
Busily seeking with a continual change.

Thanked be fortune it hath been otherwise
Twenty times better, but once in special,
In thin array after a pleasant guise,
When her loose gown from her shoulders did fall
And she me caught in her arms long and small,
Therewithal sweetly did me kiss
And softly said 'Dear heart, how like you this?'

It was no dream: I lay broad waking.
But all is turned thorough my gentleness
Into a strange fashion of forsaking.
And I have leave to go of her goodness
And she also to use newfangleness.
But since that I so kindly am served
I would fain know what she hath deserved.

[possibly in imitation of Ovid, *Amores* III, 7]

～

Alas, madam, for stealing of a kiss
Have I so much your mind there offended?
Have I then done so grievously amiss
That by no means it may be amended?
Then revenge you, and the next way is this:
Another kiss shall have my life ended.
For to my mouth the first my heart did suck;
The next shall clean out of my breast it pluck.

[imitated from Serafino]

~

What needeth these threatening words and wasted wind?
All this cannot make me restore my prey.
To rob your good, iwis, is not my mind,
Nor causeless your fair hand did I display.
Let Love be judge or else whom next we meet
That may both hear what you and I can say:
'She took from me an heart and I a glove from her.
Let us see now if th'one be worth th'other.'

[imitated from Serafino]

～

Th'en'my of life, decayer of all kind
That with his cold withers away the green,
This other night me in my bed did find
And offered me to rid my fever clean,
And I did grant, so did despair me blind.
He drew his bow with arrow sharp and keen
And strake the place where love had bit before
And drave the first dart deeper more and more.

My lute, awake! Perform the last
Labour that thou and I shall waste,
And end that I have now begun;
For when this song is sung and past,
My lute be still, for I have done.

As to be heard where ear is none,
As lead to grave in marble stone,
My song may pierce her heart as soon.
Should we then sigh or sing or moan?
No, no, my lute, for I have done.

The rocks do not so cruelly
Repulse the waves continually
As she my suit and affection,
So that I am past remedy,
Whereby my lute and I have done.

Proud of the spoil that thou hast got
Of simple hearts thorough Love's shot
By whom, unkind, thou hast them won,
Think not he hath his bow forgot
Although my lute and I have done.

Vengeance shall fall on thy disdain
That makest but game on earnest pain.
Think not alone under the sun
Unquit to cause thy lovers plain
Although my lute and I have done.

Perchance thee lie withered and old
The winter nights that are so cold,
Plaining in vain unto the moon.
Thy wishes then dare not be told.
Care then who list for I have done.

And then may chance thee to repent
The time that thou hast lost and spent
To cause thy lovers sigh and swoon.
Then shalt thou know beauty but lent
And wish and want as I have done.

Now cease, my lute. This is the last
Labour that thou and I shall waste
And ended is that we begun.
Now is this song both sung and past.
My lute, be still, for I have done.

∾

Nature that gave the bee so feat a grace
To find honey of so wondrous fashion
Hath taught the spider out of the same place
To fetch poison, by strange alteration.
Though this be strange, it is a stranger case
With one kiss, by secret operation,
Both these at once in those your lips to find,
In change whereof I leave my heart behind.

∾

I have sought long with steadfastness
To have had some ease of my great smart
But naught availeth faithfulness
To grave within your stony heart.

But hap and hit or else hit not
As uncertain as is the wind,
Right so it fareth by the shot
Of Love, alas, that is so blind.

Therefore I played the fool in vain
With pity when I first began
Your cruel heart for to constrain,
Since love regardeth no doleful man.

But of your goodness all your mind
Is that I should complain in vain.
This is the favour that I find:
Ye list to hear how I can plain.

But though I plain to please your heart,
Trust me I trust to temper it so
Not for to care which do revert:
All shall be one in wealth or woe.

For fancy ruleth though right say nay,
Even as the good man kissed his cow:
None other reason can ye lay
But as who sayeth, 'I reck not how.'

In aeternum I was once determed
For to have loved, and my mind affirmed
That with my heart it should be confirmed
　In aeternum.

Forthwith I found the thing that I might like
And sought with love to warm her heart alike,
For as me thought I should not see the like
　In aeternum.

To trace this dance I put myself in press.
Vain hope did lead and bade I should not cease
To serve, to suffer, and still to hold my peace
　In aeternum.

With this first rule I furthered me apace
That, as methought, my troth had taken place
With full assurance to stand in her grace
　In aeternum.

It was not long ere I by proof had found
That feeble building is on feeble ground;
For in her heart this word did never sound:
　In aeternum.

In aeternum then from my heart I cast
That I had first determined for the best.
Now in the place another thought doth rest
　In aeternum.

~

Though this thy port and I thy servant true
And thou thyself dost cast thy beams from high
From thy chief house, promising to renew
Both joy and eke delight, behold yet how that I,
Banished from my bliss, carefully do cry,
'Help now, Cytherea my lady dear,
My fearful trust *en voguant la galère*.'

Alas, the doubt that dreadful absence giveth!
Without thine aid assurance is there none.
The firm faith that in the water fleeteth
Succour thou therefore; in thee it is alone.
Stay that with faith that faithfully doth moan
And thou also givest me both hope and fear.
Remember thou me *en voguant la galère*.

By seas and hills elonged from thy sight,
Thy wonted grace reducing to my mind,
In stead of sleep thus I occupy the night.
A thousand thoughts and many doubts I find
And still I trust thou canst not be unkind,
Or else despair my comfort, and my cheer
Would flee forthwith *en voguant la galère*.

Yet, on my faith, full little doth remain
Of any hope whereby I may myself uphold,
For since that only words do me retain
I may well think thy affection is but cold.
But since my will is nothing as I would
But in thy hands it resteth whole and clear,
Forget me not *en voguant la galère*.

en voguant la galère – while rowing the galley

34

Unstable dream, according to the place,
Be steadfast once or else at least be true.
By tasted sweetness make me not to rue
The sudden loss of thy false feigned grace.
By good respect in such a dangerous case
Thou brought'st not her into this tossing mew
But madest my sprite live my care to renew,
My body in tempest her succour to embrace.
The body dead, the sprite had his desire;
Painless was th'one, th'other in delight.
Why then, alas, did it not keep it right,
Returning to leap into the fire,
And where it was at wish it could not remain?
Such mocks of dreams they turn to deadly pain.

[possibly imitated from Filosseno]

Process of time worketh such wonder
That water which is of kind so soft
Doth pierce the marble stone asunder
By little drops falling from aloft.

And yet an heart that seems so tender
Receiveth no drop of the stilling tears
That alway still cause me to render
The vain plaint that sounds not in her ears.

So cruel, alas, is naught alive,
So fierce, so froward, so out of frame,
But some way, some time may so contrive
By means the wild to temper and tame.

And I that always have sought and seek
Each place, each time, for some lucky day,
This fierce tiger, less I find her meek
And more denied the longer I pray.

The lion in his raging furor
Forbears that sueth meekness, for his boot;
And thou, alas, in extreme dolour
The heart so low thou treads under thy foot.

Each fierce thing, lo, how thou dost exceed
And hides it under so humble a face.
And yet the humble to help at need–
Naught helpeth time, humbleness, nor place.

The lively sparks that issue from those eyes
Against the which ne vaileth no defence
Have pressed mine heart and done it none offence
With quaking pleasure more than once or twice.
Was never man could anything devise
The sunbeams to turn with so great vehemence
To daze man's sight, as by their bright presence
Dazed am I, much like unto the guise
Of one eye-stricken with dint of lightning,
Blinded with the stroke, erring here and there.
So call I for help, I not when ne where,
The pain of my fall patiently bearing.
For after the blaze, as is no wonder,
Of deadly 'Nay' hear I the fearful thunder.

[imitated from Petrarch, *Rime* CCLVIII]

If waker care, if sudden pale colour,
If many sighs, with little speech to plain,
Now joy, now woe, if they my cheer distain,
For hope of small, if much to fear therefore,
To haste, to slack my pace less or more
Be sign of love, then do I love again.
If thou ask whom, sure since I did refrain
Her that did set our country in a roar,
Th'unfeigned cheer of Phyllis hath the place
That Brunet had. She hath and ever shall.
She from myself now hath me in her grace.
She hath in hand my wit, my will and all.
My heart alone well worthy she doth stay
Without whose help scant do I live a day.

You that in love find luck and abundance
And live in lust and joyful jollity,
Arise for shame, do away your sluggardy,
Arise, I say, do May some observance!
Let me in bed lie dreaming in mischance,
Let me remember the haps most unhappy
That me betide in May most commonly,
As one whom love list little to avance.
Sephame said true that my nativity
Mischanced was with the ruler of the May.
He guessed, I prove of that the verity:
In May my wealth and eke my life, I say,
Have stood so oft in such perplexity.
Rejoice! Let me dream of your felicity.

~

Tagus, farewell, that westward with thy streams
Turns up the grains of gold already tried
With spur and sail, for I go seek the Thames,
Gainward the sun that shew'th her wealthy pride
And, to the town which Brutus sought by dreams,
Like bended moon doth lend her lusty side.
My king, my country, alone for whom I live,
Of mighty love the wings for this me give.

Mine own John Poyntz, since ye delight to know
    The cause why that homeward I me draw
    And flee the press of courts whereso they go
Rather than to live thrall under the awe
    Of lordly looks wrapped within my cloak
    To will and lust learning to set a law
It is not because I scorn or mock
    The power of them to whom Fortune hath lent
    Charge over us, of right to strike the stroke;
But true it is that I have always meant
    Less to esteem them than the common sort,
    Of outward things that judge in their intent
Without regard what doth inward resort.
    I grant sometime that of glory the fire
    Doth touch my heart; me list to report
Blame by honour and honour to desire.
    But how may I this honour now attain
    That cannot dye the colour black a liar?
My Poyntz, I cannot frame my tongue to feign
    To cloak the truth for praise, without desert,
    Of them that list all vice for to retain.
I cannot honour them that sets their part
    With Venus and Bacchus all their life long,
    Nor hold my peace of them although I smart.
I cannot crouch nor kneel to do such wrong
    To worship them like God on earth alone
    That are like wolves these silly lambs among.
I cannot with my words complain and moan
    And suffer nought, nor smart without complaint,
    Nor turn the word that from my mouth is gone.
I cannot speak and look like a saint,
    Use wiles for wit and make deceit a pleasure
    And call craft counsel, for profit still to paint.

I cannot wrest the law to fill the coffer,
>With innocent blood to feed myself fat,
>And do most hurt where most help I offer.
I am not he that can allow the state
>Of him Caesar and damn Cato to die,
>That with his death did scape out of the gate
From Caesar's hands, if Livy doth not lie,
>And would not live where liberty was lost,
>So did his heart the common wealth apply.
I am not he such eloquence to boast
>To make the crow singing as the swan,
>Nor call the lion of coward beasts the most
That cannot take a mouse as the cat can;
>And he that dieth for hunger of the gold,
>Call him Alexander, and say that Pan
Passeth Apollo in music many fold;
>Praise Sir Thopas for a noble tale
>And scorn the story that the knight told;
Praise him for counsel that is drunk of ale;
>Grin when he laugheth that beareth all the sway,
>Frown when he frowneth and groan when he is pale,
On other's lust to hang both night and day.
>None of these points would ever frame in me.
>My wit is naught. I cannot learn the way.
And much the less of things that greater be,
>That asken help of colours of device
>To join the mean with each extremity:
With the nearest virtue to cloak away the vice
>And, as to purpose likewise it shall fall,
>To press the virtue that it may not rise.
As drunkenness good fellowship to call;
>The friendly foe with his double face
>Say he is gentle and courteous therewithal;
And say that Favel hath a goodly grace
>In eloquence; and cruelty to name
>Zeal of justice and change in time and place;

And he that suffereth offence without blame
    Call him pitiful, and him true and plain
    That raileth reckless to every man's shame;
Say he is rude that cannot lie and feign,
    The lecher a lover, and tyranny
    To be the right of a prince's reign.
I cannot, I! No, no, it will not be!
    This is the cause that I could never yet
    Hang on their sleeves that weigh, as thou mayst see,
A chip of chance more than a pound of wit.
    This maketh me at home to hunt and to hawk
    And in foul weather at my book to sit;
In frost and snow then with my bow to stalk.
    No man doth mark whereso I ride or go;
    In lusty leas in liberty I walk.
And of these news I feel nor weal nor woe,
    Save that a clog doth hang yet at my heel.
    No force for that, for it is ordered so
That I may leap both hedge and dike full well.
    I am not now in France to judge the wine,
    With savoury sauce the delicates to feel;
Nor yet in Spain where one must him incline,
    Rather than to be, outwardly to seem.
    I meddle not with wits that be so fine.
Nor Flander's cheer letteth not my sight to deem
    Of black and white nor taketh my wit away
    With beastliness they, beasts, do so esteem.
Nor am I not where Christ is given in prey
    For money, poison, and treason at Rome –
    A common practice used night and day.
But here I am in Kent and Christendom
    Among the Muses where I read and rhyme,
    Where if thou list, my Poyntz, for to come,
Thou shalt be judge how I do spend my time.

A spending hand that alway poureth out
    Had need to have a bringer-in as fast;
    And On the stone that still doth turn about
There groweth no moss – these proverbs yet do last.
    Reason hath set them in so sure a place
    That length of years their force can never waste.
When I remember this and eke the case
    Wherein thou stands, I thought forthwith to write,
    Brian, to thee, who knows how great a grace
In writing is to counsel man the right,
    To thee therefore that trots still up and down
    And never rests but running day and night
From realm to realm, from city, street, and town.
    Why dost thou wear thy body to the bones
    And mightst at home sleep in thy bed of down
And drink good ale so nappy for the nonce,
    Feed thyself fat and heap up pound by pound?
    Likest thou not this? 'No.' Why? 'For swine so groins
In sty and chaw the turds moulded on the ground,
    And drivel on pearls, the head still in the manger.
    Then of the harp the ass do hear the sound.
So sacks of dirt be filled up in the cloister
    That serves for less than do these fatted swine.
    Though I seem lean and dry without moisture,
Yet will I serve my prince, my lord and thine,
    And let them live to feed the paunch that list,
    So I may feed to live, both me and mine.'
By God, well said, but what and if thou wist
    How to bring in as fast as thou dost spend?
    'That would I learn.' And it shall not be missed
To tell thee how. Now hark what I intend.
    Thou know'st well, first, whoso can seek to please
    Shall purchase friends where truth shall but offend.

Flee therefore truth: it is both wealth and ease.
  For though that truth of every man hath praise,
  Full near that wind goeth truth in great misease.
Use virtue as it goeth now-a-days,
  In word alone to make thy language sweet,
  And of the deed yet do not as thou says.
Else be thou sure thou shalt be far unmeet
  To get thy bread, each thing is now so scant.
  Seek still thy profit upon thy bare feet.
Lend in no wise, for fear that thou do want,
  Unless it be as to a dog a cheese;
  By which return be sure to win a cant
Of half at least – it is not good to leese.
  Learn at Kitson, that in a long white coat
  From under the stall without lands or fees
Hath leapt into the shop; who knoweth by rote
  This rule that I have told thee herebefore.
  Sometime also rich age beginneth to dote;
See thou when there thy gain may be the more.
  Stay him by the arm whereso he walk or go.
  Be near alway and, if he cough too sore,
When he hath spit, tread out and please him so.
  A diligent knave that picks his master's purse
  May please him so that he, withouten moe,
Executor is, and what is he the worse?
  But if so chance you get naught of the man,
  The widow may for all thy charge deburse.
A rivelled skin, a stinking breath, what then?
  A toothless mouth shall do thy lips no harm.
  The gold is good, and though she curse or ban,
Yet where thee list thou mayst lie good and warm:
  Let the old mule bite upon the bridle
  Whilst there do lie a sweeter in thine arm.
In this also see you be not idle:
  Thy niece, thy cousin, thy sister, or thy daughter,
  If she be fair, if handsome be her middle,

If thy better hath her love besought her,
    Advance his cause and he shall help thy need.
    It is but love. Turn it to a laughter.
But ware, I say, so gold thee help and speed
    That in this case thou be not so unwise
    As Pandar was in such a like deed;
For he, the fool, of conscience was so nice
    That he no gain would have for all his pain.
    Be next thyself, for friendship bears no prize.
Laugh'st thou at me? Why? Do I speak in vain?
    'No, not at thee, but at thy thrifty jest.
    Wouldest thou I should for any loss or gain
Change that for gold that I have ta'en for best—
    Next godly things, to have an honest name?
    Should I leave that? Then take me for a beast!'
Nay then, farewell, and if you care for shame,
    Content thee then with honest poverty,
    With free tongue, what thee mislikes, to blame,
And, for thy truth, sometime adversity.
    And therewithal this thing I shall thee give—
    In this world now, little prosperity,
And coin to keep, as water in a sieve.

from Psalm 32

O diverse are the chastisings of sin:
In meat, in drink, in breath that man doth blow,
In sleep, in watch, in fretting still within
    That never suffer rest unto the mind
    Filled with offence, that new and new begin
With thousand fears the heart to strain and bind.
    But for all this he that in God doth trust
    With mercy shall himself defended find.
Joy and rejoice, I say, ye that be just,
    In him that mak'th and holdeth you so still.
    In him your glory alway set you must,
All ye that be of upright heart and will.

from Psalm 102

Lord, hear my prayer and let my cry pass
   Unto thee, Lord, without impediment.
   Do not from me turn thy merciful face,
Unto myself leaving my government.
   In time of trouble and adversity
   Incline to me thine ear and thine intent.
And when I call, help my necessity,
   Readily grant th'effect of my desire.
   These bold demands do please thy majesty
And eke my case such haste doth well require.
   For like as smoke my days been passed away,
   My bones dried up as furnace with the fire.
My heart, my mind is withered up like hay
   Because I have forgot to take my bread,
   My bread of life, the word of truth, I say.
And for my plaintful sighes and my dread,
   My bones, my strength, my very force of mind
   Cleaved to the flesh and from thy sprite were fled
As desperate thy mercy for to find.
   So made I me the solein pelican
   And like the owl that fleeth by proper kind
Light of the day and hath herself beta'en
   To ruin life out of all company,
   With waker care that with this woe began,
Like the sparrow was I solitary
   That sits alone under the house's eaves.

from Psalm 130

From depth of sin and from a deep despair,
　　From depth of death, from depth of heart's sorrow,
　　From this deep cave of darkness' deep repair,
Thee have I called, O Lord, to be my borrow.
　　Thou in my voice, O Lord, perceive and hear
　　My heart, my hope, my plaint, my overthrow,
My will to rise, and let by grant appear
　　That to my voice thine ears do well intend.
　　No place so far that to thee is not near;
No depth so deep that thou ne mayst extend
　　Thine ear thereto. Hear then my woeful plaint.

∾

A face that should content me wondrous well
Should not be fair but comely to behold,
With gladsome look all grief for to expel,
With sober cheer so would I that it should
Speak, without words, such words that none can tell.
The tress also should be of crisped gold.
With wit and these, might chance I might be tied
And knit again the knot that should not slide.

Driven to desire, adread also to dare,
Between two stools my tail goeth to the ground.
Dread and desire the reason doth confound,
The tongue put to silence. The heart, in hope and fear,
Doth dread that it dare and hide that would appear.
Desirous and dreadful, at liberty I go bound.
For pressing to proffer methinks I hear the sound:
Back off thy boldness. Thy courage passeth care.
This dangerous doubt, whether to obey
My dread or my desire, so sore doth me trouble
That cause causeth for dread of my decay.
In thought all one; in deeds to show me double,
Fearful and faithful! Yet take me as I am,
Though double in deeds, an inward perfect man.

Horrible of hue, hideous to behold,
Careful of countenance, his hair all clustered,
With dead droppy blood that down his face rolled,
Pale, painful, and piteously pierced,
His heart in sunder sorrowfully shivered,
Methought a man, thus marvellously murdered,
This night to me came and carefully cried:

'O man misfortunate, more than any creature,
That painfully yet lives more pain to perceive,
What hardened hath thy heart this harm to suffer?
Thy doubtful hope, it do thee but deceive.
No good nor grace to glad thee shalt receive.
By pain from thy pain then pain to procure,
Moe bitter it were than death to endure.

'Follow me,' saith he, 'hold here my hand.
Too long is death in tears to groan.
The sea shall sooner quench the brand
Of the desire that hath thee thus undone
Or sooner send thee to a deadly swoon.
Hold in thy hand the haft here of this knife
And with the blade boldly bereave thy life.

'Come off,' quod he. 'I come,' quod I.
Then therewith as methought
My breast I pierced painfully.
My heart right soon I it raught.
But, lord, alas, it was for naught
For with that stroke I did awake.
My heart for sorrow yet feel I quake.

I am as I am and so will I be
But how that I am none knoweth truly.
Be it evil, be it well, be I bound, be I free,
I am as I am and so will I be.

I lead my life indifferently,
I mean no thing but honestly.
And though folks judge full diversely
I am as I am and so will I die.

I do not rejoice nor yet complain.
Both mirth and sadness I do refrain
And use the mean since folks will feign.
Yet I am as I am, be it pleasure or pain.

Diverse do judge as they do trow,
Some of pleasure and some of woe.
Yet for all that, nothing they know.
But I am as I am wheresoever I go.

But since that judgers do thus decay
Let every man his judgement say.
I will it take in sport and play
For I am as I am whosoever say nay.

Who judgeth well, well God him send.
Who judgeth evil, God them amend.
To judge the best therefore intend
For I am as I am and so will I end.

Yet some there be that take delight
To judge folks' thought for envy and spite.
But whether they judge me wrong or right
I am as I am and so do I write,

Praying you all that this do read
To trust it as you do your creed
And not to think I change my weed
For I am as I am however I speed.

But how that is I leave to you.
Judge as ye list, false or true.
Ye know no more than afore ye knew.
Yet I am as I am whatever ensue.

And from this mind I will not flee,
But to you all that misjudge me
I do protest, as ye may see,
That I am as I am and so will I be.

In mourning wise since daily I increase,
Thus should I cloak the cause of all my grief:
So pensive mind with tongue to hold his peace.
My reason sayeth there can be no relief;
Wherefore give ear, I humbly you require,
The affects to know that thus doth make me moan.
The cause is great of all my doleful cheer
For those that were and now be dead and gone.

What though to death desert be now their call
As by their faults it doth appear right plain.
Of force I must lament that such a fall
Should light on those so wealthily did reign,
Though some perchance will say, of cruel heart,
'A traitor's death why should we thus bemoan?'
But I, alas, set this offence apart,
Must needs bewail the death of some be gone.

As for them all I do not thus lament
But as of right my reason doth me bind.
But as the most doth all their deaths repent,
Even so do I by force of mourning mind.
Some say, 'Rochford, hadst thou been not so proud,
For thy great wit each man would thee bemoan.'
Since as it is so, many cry aloud
'It is great loss that thou art dead and gone.'

Ah, Norris, Norris, my tears begin to run
To think what hap did thee so lead or guide,
Whereby thou hast both thee and thine undone,
That is bewailed in court of every side.
In place also where thou hast never been
Both man and child doth piteously thee moan.
They say, 'Alas, thou art far overseen
By thine offences to be thus dead and gone.'

55

Ah, Weston, Weston, that pleasant was and young,
In active things who might with thee compare?
All words accept that thou didst speak with tongue,
So well esteemed with each where thou didst fare.
And we that now in court doth lead our life,
Most part in mind doth thee lament and moan.
But that thy faults we daily hear so rife,
All we should weep that thou art dead and gone.

Brereton, farewell, as one that least I knew.
Great was thy love with diverse, as I hear,
But common voice doth not so sore thee rue
As other twain that doth before appear.
But yet no doubt but thy friends thee lament
And other hear their piteous cry and moan.
So doth each heart for thee likewise relent
That thou giv'st cause thus to be dead and gone.

Ah, Mark, what moan should I for thee make more
Since that thy death thou hast deserved best,
Save only that mine eye is forced sore
With piteous plaint to moan thee with the rest?
A time thou hadst above thy poor degree,
The fall whereof thy friends may well bemoan.
A rotten twig upon so high a tree
Hath slipped thy hold and thou art dead and gone.

And thus, farewell, each one in hearty wise.
The axe is home, your heads be in the street.
The trickling tears doth fall so from my eyes,
I scarce may write, my paper is so wet.
But what can help when death hath played his part
Though nature's course will thus lament and moan?
Leave sobs therefore and every Christian heart
Pray for the souls of those be dead and gone.

Quondam was I in my lady's grace,
I think as well as now be you
And when that you have trod the trace
Then shall you know my words be true,
 That *quondam* was I.

Quondam was I. She said for ever.
That 'ever' lasted but a short while.
Promise made not to dissever,
I thought she laughed – she did but smile.
 Then *quondam* was I.

Quondam was I – he that full oft lay
In her arms with kisses many one.
It is enough that this I may say:
Though among the moe now I be gone
 Yet *quondam* was I.

Quondam was I. Yet she will you tell
That, since the hour she was first born,
She never loved none half so well
As you. But what although she had sworn?
 Sure *quondam* was I.

quondam – once

She that should most, perceiveth least
The unfeigned sufferance of my great smart.
It is to her sport to have me oppressed.
But they of such life which be expert
Say that I burn uncertain in my heart.
But where judge ye? No more! Ye know not.
Ye are to blame to say I came too late.

Too late? Nay, too soon methink rather,
Thus to be entreated and have served faithfully.
Lo, thus am I rewarded among the other.
I, though unvised which was too busy,
For fear of too late I came too hastily.
But thither I came not; yet came I for all that.
But whithersoever I came, I came too late.

Who hath more cause to plain than I?
There as I am judged, too late I came;
And there as I came, I came too hastily.
Thus may I plain as I that am
Misjudged, misentreated more than any man.
Now judge, let see, of this debate,
Whether I came too hastily or too late.

Thou sleepest fast and I with woeful heart
Stand here alone, sighing and cannot fly.
Thou sleepest fast when cruel love his dart
On me doth cast, alas, so painfully.
Thou sleepest fast and I, all full of smart,
To thee, my foe, in vain do call and cry.
And yet, methinks, thou that sleepest fast,
Thou dreamest still which way my life to waste.

[imitated from Serafino]

With serving still
This I have won:
For my good will
To be undone.

And for redress
Of all my pain
Disdainfulness
I have again.

And for reward
Of all my smart,
Lo, thus unheard,
I must depart.

Wherefore all ye
That after shall
By fortune be,
As I am, thrall,

Example take
What I have won:
Thus for her sake
To be undone.

～

Who list his wealth and ease retain,
Himself let him unknown contain.
Press not too fast in at that gate
Where the return stands by disdain,
For sure, *circa Regna tonat*.

The high mountains are blasted oft
When the low valley is mild and soft.
Fortune with Health stands at debate.
The fall is grievous from aloft.
And sure, *circa Regna tonat*.

These bloody days have broken my heart.
My lust, my youth did them depart,
And blind desire of estate.
Who hastes to climb seeks to revert.
Of truth, *circa Regna tonat*.

The bell tower showed me such sight
That in my head sticks day and night.
There did I learn out of a grate,
For all favour, glory, or might,
That yet *circa Regna tonat*.

By proof, I say, there did I learn:
Wit helpeth not defence too yerne,
Of innocency to plead or prate.
Bear low, therefore, give God the stern,
For sure, *circa Regna tonat*.

circa Regna tonat – it thunders around thrones

∾

Is it possible
That so high debate,
So sharp, so sore, and of such rate,
Should end so soon and was begun so late?
Is it possible?

Is it possible
So cruel intent,
So hasty heat and so soon spent,
From love to hate and thence for to relent?
Is it possible?

Is it possible
That any may find
Within one heart do diverse mind
To change or turn as weather and wind?
Is it possible?

Is it possible
To spy it in an eye
That turns as oft as chance on die?
The truth whereof can any try?
Is it possible?

It is possible
For to turn so oft,
To bring that lowest that was most aloft
And to fall highest yet to light soft.
It is possible.

All is possible
Whoso list believe.
Trust therefore first and after preve,
As men wed ladies by licence and leave,
All is possible.

I abide and abide and better abide
And after the old proverb the happy day.
And ever my lady to me doth say
Let me alone and I will provide.
I abide and abide and tarry the tide
And with abiding speed well ye may.
Thus do I abide, I wot, alway,
Neither obtaining nor yet denied.
Aye me, this long abiding
Seemeth to me, as who saith,
A prolonging of a dying death
Or a refusing of a desired thing.
Much were it better for to be plain
Than to say Abide and yet shall not obtain.

~

Forget not yet the tried intent
Of such a truth as I have meant,
My great travail so gladly spent.
   Forget not yet,

Forget not yet when first began
The weary life ye know since when,
The suit, the service none can tell.
   Forget not yet.

Forget not yet the great assays,
The cruel wrong, the scornful ways,
The painful patience in denays.
   Forget not yet.

Forget not yet, forget not this:
How long ago hath been and is
The mind that never meant amiss.
   Forget not yet.

Forget not then thine own approved
The which so long hath thee so loved
Whose steadfast faith yet never moved.
   Forget not this.

Fortune doth frown.
What remedy?
I am down
By destiny.

❧

What thing is that that I both have and lack,
With goodwill granted and yet is denied?
How may I be received and put aback
Alwey doing and yet unoccupied?
Most slow in that I have most applied.
Thus may I say I lose all that I win,
And that that was ready is new to begin.

In wilful riches I have found poverty
And in great pleasure I lived in heaviness.
In too much freedom I lacked liberty.
Nothing but plenty caused my scarceness.
Thus was I both in joy and in distress.
And, in few words if I should be plain,
In a paradise I suffered all this pain.

~

The pillar perished is whereto I leant,
The strongest stay of mine unquiet mind.
The like of it no man again can find—
From east to west still seeking though he went—
To mine unhap, for hap away hath rent
Of all my joy the very bark and rind
And I, alas, by chance am thus assigned
Dearly to mourn till death do it relent.
But since that thus it is by destiny,
What can I more but have a woeful heart,
My pen in plaint, my voice in woeful cry,
My mind in woe, my body full of smart,
And I myself myself always to hate
Till dreadful death do ease my doleful state?

[imitated from Petrarch, *Rime* CCLXIX]

∾

A lady gave me a gift she had not
And I received her gift I took not.
She gave it me willingly and yet she would not
And I received it, albeit I could not.
If she gave it me, I force not
And if she take it again, she cares not.
Construe what is this and tell not,
For I am fast sworn I may not.

Stand whoso list upon the slipper top
Of court's estates, and let me here rejoice
And use me quiet without let or stop,
Unknown in court that hath such brackish joys.
In hidden place so let my days forth pass
That when my years be done, withouten noise.
I may die aged after the common trace.
For him death grip'th right hard by the crop
That is much known of other, and of himself, alas,
Doth die unknown, dazed, with dreadful face.